Catastrophic Storms

by Michael Sandler

TABLE OF CONTENTS

Introduction

The sky turns red. Tree branches begin to sway. Dark clouds race across the sky. Then the first drops of rain begin to fall. The storm has arrived.

An ordinary storm can ruin a picnic or a baseball game. But usually the damage from the storm is slight. A **catastrophic** (ka-tuh-STRAH-fik) storm, on the other hand, is something far, far worse.

A catastrophic storm can shut down highways, airports, and train systems. It can tear buildings from their foundations. It can lift boats out of the ocean and hurl them onto shore. Even worse, a catastrophic storm can kill hundreds, or even thousands, of people. Whole cities have been flattened to the ground by the most powerful catastrophic storms.

Hurricanes, tornadoes, and blizzards are three types of storms that can become catastrophic. Hurricanes can be the most destructive storms on our planet. They begin at sea, but do most of their damage in **coastal areas**, where the ocean meets the land. Tornadoes are smaller, but can be even more violent. They last a short time, but they produce the strongest winds that blow across Earth. Blizzards can bury whole sections of a country in a blinding mix of wind, cold, and snow.

Meteorologists (mee-tee-uh-RAH-luh-jists), the scientists who study weather, can't prevent monster storms. But every day they learn more and more about the causes and effects of these storms.

As you read, pay attention to the conditions that produce each type of storm. Notice the seasons and places in which they strike. Discover how strong each storm can become. Learn how they do their damage to land, to property, and to human life.

▲ snowstorm in Bodie, California

Hurricanes

What is a Hurricane?

A hurricane is a huge storm with heavy rain and strong winds. It is far more serious than an ordinary thunderstorm. The difference between the two is like the difference between an anthill and Mount Everest. A thunderstorm may cover an area up to 2 miles (3.2 kilometers) wide. A hurricane can cover hundreds or thousands of square miles. A thunderstorm usually lasts for an hour or so. A hurricane may last for a week or longer.

An everyday thunderstorm may have winds of 20 miles (32 kilometers) per hour. Some hurricanes have winds of 150 miles (241 kilometers) per hour or even higher.

IT'S A Fact

The word *hurricane* comes from the Caribbean Islands, where the storms often hit. The Carib Indians used the word *urican*, which means "big wind." The Taino (tie-EE-noh) people used *hurucan*, which means "evil spirit." In other parts of the world, hurricanes have different names. They are called cyclones in India. In the western Pacific Ocean they are called typhoons; in Australia they are nicknamed willie willies.

▲ A person struggles to walk in Hurricane Andrew.

Hurricanes don't just happen anywhere. They begin over the warm ocean water found on either side of the equator. Hurricanes can travel for hundreds of miles over the ocean until they hit coastal areas. This is called making **landfall**.

Hurricanes don't just happen at any time of the year. The hurricane season in the Northern Hemisphere lasts from June through November. The hurricane season in the Southern Hemisphere lasts from November through April.

▲ Hurricanes that strike the United States usually begin off the coast of Africa.

How a Hurricane Is Born

1 High-Pressure Area	2 Low-Pressure Area	3 Storm Clouds	4 Spiral	5 Strong Winds
Air warms up and collects moisture as it moves down toward the surface of the ocean.	Warm, moist air from a high-pressure area moves into the low-pressure area. The air rises and cools. More air moves in to take the rising air's place.	Water droplets in the rising air collect and form storm clouds.	Because of the rotation of Earth, storm clouds spin up in a spiral.	Air flows into the storm clouds from the bottom and from the top. This flowing air creates strong winds.

When the winds near the center of a storm blow between 23–39 miles (27–62.8 kilometers) per hour, it is called a tropical depression. If the winds grow to between 39–73 miles (62.8–117.5 kilometers) per hour, it is called a tropical storm. If the winds reach 74 miles (119 kilometers) per hour, a hurricane is born.

How Hurricanes Form

Scientists know the conditions needed for a hurricane. One condition is warm ocean water of at least 80° Fahrenheit (27° Celsius). That's why hurricanes have seasons. Ocean waters only heat up enough at certain times of the year. The other condition is low air pressure. Air near Earth's surface is always under pressure.

The pressure comes from the **atmosphere** (AT-muh-sfeer), the layers of gases that surround Earth. When the atmosphere's weight pushes down with greater force, surface air gets squeezed more. This is called high pressure. When the atmosphere pushes down with less force, surface air can rise more easily. This is called low pressure.

1. Solve This

A tropical depression has winds of 25 miles (40.2 kilometers) per hour. The storm grows stronger. A day later, winds are blowing 40 miles (64 kilometers) per hour faster. What is the storm now? Is it a tropical depression, a tropical storm, or a hurricane?

Math ☑ Point

What steps did you follow to answer the question?

Now you know how a hurricane is born. The diagram below shows you its parts.

Inside a Hurricane

Spiral Bands	Eyewall	Eye
The **spiral bands** are areas of clouds, wind, and rain that extend further out from the center of a hurricane.	Surrounding the eye is the **eyewall**, the storm's strongest part. It is a wall of swirling clouds. Here, the hurricane's fiercest winds blow and the heaviest rain falls.	At a hurricane's center is the **eye**. It is a cloudless area where the winds are somewhat calm.

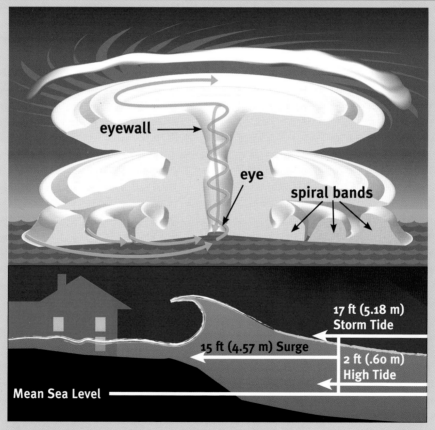

Ocean Bulge
A hurricane also affects the water below it. Winds whip up the waves. Low pressure at the storm's center pulls up on the water, creating the ocean bulge. When these bulging waters hit shore, it is called a **storm surge**.

Catastrophic Hurricanes

Scientists use a scale to measure the intensity, or strength, of a hurricane. The Saffir-Simpson scale has five levels. The levels, or categories, are based on wind speed and storm surge height. A hurricane of category 3 or higher can be truly catastrophic.

The winds from a category 3 or higher hurricane can rip trees out of the ground and hurl them through the air. They can tear the roofs off houses. They can completely destroy mobile homes. The storm surge can smash anything in its path when it hits the coast. Rain causes more damage. The ground can become soaked with more water than it can hold. Whole areas are flooded. Mudslides roar down from the sides of hills.

IT'S A
Fact

Storm surges account for about ninety percent of all hurricane-related deaths.

Category	Wind Speed in mph (kph)	Surge Height in feet (meters)
1	74–95 mph (119–153 kph)	4–5 feet (1.22–1.82 meters)
2	96–110 mph (154–177 kph)	6–8 feet (1.83–2.73 meters)
3	111–130 mph (178–209 kph)	9–12 feet (2.74–3.95 meters)
4	131–155 mph (210–250 kph)	13–18 feet (3.96–5.49 meters)
5	156+ mph (251+ kph)	18+ feet (5.49+ meters)

Hurricane Katrina, 2005

The third deadliest hurricane in United States history killed over 1,000 people and animals. It caused billions of dollars of damage in Louisiana, Alabama, Mississippi, and Florida. No one knows how long it will take to rebuild. Here is the story of the storm.

▼ New Orleans before Hurricane Katrina

▲ New Orleans after Hurricane Katrina

August 24: Meteorologists start to track tropical storm Katrina over the central Bahamas. They issue a hurricane warning to people living on the southeast coast of Florida.

August 25: Katrina becomes a category 1 hurricane. The storm hits Florida with winds of eighty miles per hour. Eleven people are killed in the storm.

August 27: Katrina becomes a category 3 storm. Its winds are 115 mph. The mayor of New Orleans urges everyone to leave the city. The concern is that the waters of Lake Ponchartrain will break through the levees. Levees are huge walls built to protect land from flooding. As people rush to evacuate, the highways are jammed with cars.

August 28: Katrina becomes a category 5 storm. Shelters are set up for people who can't leave New Orleans.

Thousands head for the Superdome football stadium to wait out the storm. Evacuation orders are also issued by the governor of Mississippi for all the towns and cities along the coast.

August 29: Katrina makes landfall as a category 4 storm near Buras, Louisiana, a little after 7:00 A.M. The winds are so strong that they rip holes in the roof of the Superdome where more than 10,000 families have camped out.

August 30: In the wake of the winds and storm surge, two of the levees on Lake Ponchartrain break. Water pours out, and in a matter of hours, more than eighty percent of New Orleans is under water. In some places the water is more than twenty feet high. People scramble to rooftops and higher ground to try to get away from the quickly rising waters.

After Katrina

August 31: In the Gulf of Mexico, five oil rigs are reported missing. Two more have broken free from their anchors.

September 1: More than 50,000 people are in Red Cross shelters. Close to 30,000 people are in the New Orleans Superdome. With thousands of people without water, food, or electricity, violence breaks out around the city. Stores are looted for food, diapers, and other goods. Hospitals have no electricity and doctors plead for help for the sick. Without medical care, many are dying.

▲ homes in Louisiana destroyed by Hurricane Katrina

IT'S A

Fact

To track hurricanes, meteorologists give each tropical storm a name. The first storm of the season gets a name beginning with the letter A. The second gets a name that begins with the letter B. The process continues through the alphabet. For many years, hurricanes were only given women's names. Since 1979, men's names have also been used.

What's Next?

September 2: President Bush tours the area and admits that the government has not acted fast enough and people are suffering because of this. He promises to get more help as fast as possible.

The final death toll of Hurricane Katrina was 1,836 people, with 705 still missing. About 600,000 pets were killed or left homeless. Reports put the loss of homes along the Gulf Coast at 275,000, and the total cost of the hurricane at about $110 billion in damages.

2. Solve This

Use the table below to answer the following question.

Is the following statement true or false? Before Katrina, Hurricane Andrew caused more damage than hurricanes Hugo, Agnes, Betsy, and Camille combined.

Hurricane	Year	Category	Damage*
Andrew	1992	5	$34,955,000,000
Hugo	1989	4	$ 9,740,000,000
Agnes	1972	1	$ 8,621,000,000
Betsy	1965	3	$ 8,517,000,000
Camille	1969	5	$ 6,992,000,000

*rounded to the nearest million dollars

Tornadoes

What Is a Tornado?

A tornado is a severe windstorm. It is a rotating, or spinning, column of air. It can look like a long, thin tube or a big spinning funnel. Often, it is wider on top and narrower near the ground. A tornado is often called a twister. That's because of its twisting, spinning motion.

These twisting columns of air may be hard to see at first. But as the air twists, it sucks up dirt and dust. The whirling dirt and dust make a tornado look gray or even black.

The noise a tornado makes can be even more frightening than how it looks. Many compare it to the sound of a freight train roaring down the tracks.

A tornado is much smaller than a hurricane, usually measuring less than a mile (1.6 kilometers) in width.

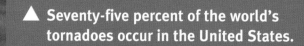
▲ Seventy-five percent of the world's tornadoes occur in the United States.

A tornado lasts a shorter time than a hurricane, generally a few minutes to an hour. It travels a shorter distance, perhaps just 200 yards (about 183 meters). But there are rare examples of a tornado traveling for 100 miles (about 161 kilometers).

The violent winds of a tornado can be stronger than a hurricane's winds. Tornado winds have been measured at 300 to 350 miles (482 to 563 kilometers) per hour.

Meteorologists can predict, or tell ahead of time, what a hurricane's path might be. They can't do the same for a tornado. A tornado may sit spinning in one spot. Or, it may tear across the ground at 60 miles (96.5 kilometers) per hour.

▲ The shaded areas show where the most tornadoes occur.

Tornadoes strike all over the world, but certain places get more than others. In the United States, tornadoes occur in every state. Most develop east of the Rocky Mountains and west of the Appalachian (ap-puh-LAY-chin) Mountains. Although a tornado can occur on any day, tornado season arrives in late spring and lasts into the summer.

IT'S A
Fact

A waterspout is a tornado that forms or passes over the water.

How Tornadoes Form

A tornado needs warm, moist air, just like a hurricane. In the United States, this is often a mass of air blowing up from the Gulf of Mexico.

This mass collides with a mass of cooler, drier air from northern areas. Thunderstorms develop where the two masses meet. Tornadoes grow out of thunderstorms.

How a Tornado Is Born

1 Cool Air

Cool air forces warm air up, creating an **updraft.**

2 Warm Air

Moisture from the warm air forms thunderclouds. Water droplets in the clouds become rain.

3

There are now downward winds from the heavy rain.

4

Near the ground, winds racing into and away from the storm create a spinning column of air.

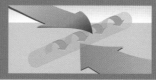

5

The updraft from the thunderstorm tilts this column up toward the sky. It becomes vertical, extending from the ground into the storm.

6

More air rushes into the column. The rotating winds get stronger. Water vapor from the falling rain creates a spinning funnel-shaped cloud. The tornado is born.

Cool Air Mass

Warm Air Mass

Catastrophic Tornadoes

To measure the strength of a tornado, scientists use the Fujita (foo-JEE-tuh) Wind Damage Scale. The scale ranks tornadoes from F0 to F5, based on their wind speed. F0 and F1 tornadoes are weak. F2 and F3 tornadoes are strong. F4 and F5 tornadoes are violent. They can do catastrophic damage.

The damage is caused by the wind. F4 and F5 tornadoes can lift up an automobile. F4 and F5 tornadoes can suck the roof off of a building and tear off its walls. F4 and F5 tornadoes can reduce a building to a pile of rubble or lift it off the ground. Though people can be sucked up by a tornado, flying objects cause most injuries and deaths.

▲ scientist Ted Fujita

Category	Wind Speed in mph (kph)	Damage
THE FUJITA SCALE		
F0	72 mph (116 kph)	**Light:** branches broken, chimneys damaged
F1	73–112 mph (117–180 kph)	**Moderate:** cars pushed off roads, mobile homes overturned
F2	113–157 mph (181–253 kph)	**Considerable:** mobile homes smashed, small objects become missiles
F3	158–206 mph (254–332 kph)	**Severe:** roofs and walls torn from well-built houses, trees uprooted, medium-size objects become missiles
F4	207–260 mph (333–418 kph)	**Devastating:** houses destroyed, large objects become missiles
F5	261–319 mph (419–513 kph)	**Incredible:** strong houses thrown through the air, cars hurled 100 yards (about 91 meters)

The Tri-State Tornado

On March 18, 1925, a fierce thunderstorm developed in the Ozark (OH-zark) Mountains in Missouri. Out of the storm burst an F5 tornado. The tornado headed northeast. It kept going for a record three and one-half hours. The tornado passed through three states on its 219-mile (342-kilometer) trip. People called it the Tri-State Tornado.

The twister tore through city after city with winds of 300 miles (482.7 kilometers) per hour. Trees, homes, and barns were sucked into the storm and hurled through the air. In all, the Tri-State Tornado killed nearly 700 people in Missouri, Illinois, and Indiana. It was the deadliest twister in American history.

▲ The Tri-State storm destroyed everything in its path.

3. Solve This

Use the bar graph at right to answer the questions.

a. What percentage of tornadoes are F4s and F5s?

b. What percentage of tornado-related deaths are caused by F4s and F5s?

c. Which categories of tornadoes cause about 30% of tornado-related deaths?

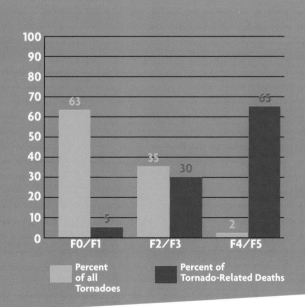

Percent of all Tornadoes

Percent of Tornado-Related Deaths

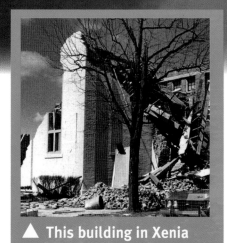

▲ This building in Xenia was ripped in half by tornadoes.

The Super Outbreak

The only thing more frightening than one tornado is a group of them. A single thunderstorm can produce a "family" of tornadoes, one after another. Certain weather conditions can produce tornado outbreaks across many states.

An outbreak of tornadoes happened on April 3, 1974. During a 24-hour period, 148 tornadoes touched down in thirteen states. At least 330 deaths were recorded. More than 5,000 were injured. This "Super Outbreak" of tornadoes caused about $600 million in damage. The worst tornado blew into the small town of Xenia, Ohio. It had winds of more than 260 miles (418 kilometers) per hour. Nearly half of the town's homes were damaged or destroyed.

The loss of life in the Super Outbreak could have been much worse. Many people were paying close attention to the weather because of a small outbreak two days earlier. When weathercasters broadcast new tornado warnings, people quickly headed for shelter.

The Wizard of Oz

What's the most famous tornado that never really happened? Probably the twister that sucked up Dorothy and her dog, Toto, and lifted them to Oz. The tornado in the famous book and movie was pure fiction. But people have been sucked up into tornadoes in real life.

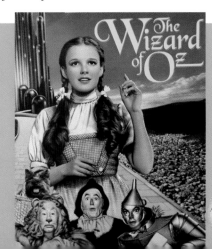

Tornado Alley

One part of the Midwest gets so many tornadoes that it's known as Tornado Alley. There are more tornadoes here than anywhere else in the world.

Why does Tornado Alley get so many twisters? Because it gets so many thunderstorms! Cold air from the Rocky Mountains can flow freely over Tornado Alley's flat plains. This cold air meets warm, moist air from the Gulf of Mexico. The resulting thunderstorms are perfect for creating tornadoes.

On May 3, 1999, more than forty twisters hit a patch of Tornado Alley in Oklahoma. President Bill Clinton declared sixteen counties disaster areas. The wind speed of one twister was measured at 318 miles (512 kilometers) per hour. These were the strongest winds ever recorded on Earth.

▼ The average tornado lasts for just seven minutes. It is most likely to strike in the late afternoon. About twenty-five percent of tornadoes occur between 4:00 P.M. and 6:00 P.M.

▼ The shaded area is Tornado Alley.

Tornado Safety

In the past, people were sometimes told to open their windows if a tornado came near. The idea was to make the air pressure inside the same as the air pressure outside. Some thought that a tornado's low pressure could cause buildings to explode.

Today, tornado experts say you should forget about opening windows. If a tornado strikes a building, it will blast the windows to pieces, open or closed. Leave the windows alone, the experts say. Instead, head for safety.

Where are the safest places? Get as far away from windows as possible! Go down to the basement, if there is one. If possible, cover yourself with thick padding such as a mattress or a few blankets.

POINT

Think About It
Which do you consider more frightening—a tornado or a hurricane? Why?

4. Solve This

The year 1992 was record-breaking for tornadoes. In the United States, 1,297 twisters were reported. Of those, 420 tornadoes struck four Tornado Alley states: Oklahoma, Texas, Nebraska, and Kansas. How many tornadoes struck in other states?

Math ☑ Point

What strategy did you use to solve the problem? Did you add, subtract, multiply, or divide?

21

Blizzards

What Is a Blizzard?

People often call any snowstorm a blizzard. A true blizzard must pass three tests. First, the storm must have winds of at least 35 miles (56.3 kilometers) per hour. Second, the temperature must be below 20° Fahrenheit (–7° Celsius). Finally, falling or blowing snow must cut a person's ability to see to a distance of a quarter mile (about .40 of a kilometer) or less.

Blizzards can occur anyplace where temperatures are cold enough for snow to form. In the United States, they often occur in the northern Great Plains. Midwestern and eastern states have also been hit by many blizzards. Some blizzards are so huge that they cover whole sections of the country. Blizzards often happen toward the beginning or end of winter.

Everyday Science

The wind of a blizzard blows heat away from a person's body. People lose heat faster than they would in nonmoving air. The effect is called **wind chill**. Low wind chill can cause **frostbite** and **hypothermia** (hy-poh-THER-mee-uh). Frostbite is a loss of feeling in the fingers, toes, or other parts of the body exposed to the cold. During hypothermia, human body temperatures become dangerously low. Hypothermia can be deadly if it is not treated quickly.

5. Solve This

Use the table below to solve the problems.

a. The temperature is 20° Fahrenheit. The winds are 35 miles per hour. What is the wind chill?

b. The temperature drops another 10 degrees and the winds speed up to 50 miles per hour. What is the wind chill now?

WIND CHILL

TEMPERATURE (degrees Fahrenheit)

	30	25	20	15	10	5	0
5	25	19	13	7	1	-5	-11
10	21	15	9	3	-4	-10	-16
15	19	13	6	0	-7	-13	**-19**
20	17	11	4	-2	-9	-15	**-22**
25	16	9	3	-4	-11	-17	**-24**
30	15	8	1	-5	-12	**-19**	**-26**
35	14	7	0	-7	-14	**-21**	**-27**
40	13	6	-1	-8	-15	**-22**	**-29**
45	12	5	-2	-9	-16	**-23**	**-30**
50	12	4	-3	-10	-17	**-24**	**-31**
55	11	4	-3	-11	**-18**	**-25**	
60	10	3	-4	-11	**-19**	**-26**	

WIND (mph)

▲ The numbers in black indicate that a person could have frostbite in about 30 minutes.

How Blizzards Form

You might think that blizzards happen all winter long in the world's coldest places. In fact, blizzards are fairly rare. The reason is the need for moisture. Cold, dry air does not produce much snow. So a blizzard needs a mixture of warm air and cold air in order to form.

How a Blizzard Is Born

1 Warm Air

A mass of warm air, coming from tropical areas, runs into a mass of cold air from a **polar** region.

2 Warm Front

The leading edge of the warm air mass is called a **warm front**. The warm front air is lighter than the colder air that it hits. So the warm air rises up above the cold air.

3 Cool Air

Water vapor in the warm air condenses in the colder air in the clouds. Then it falls as snow.

cool air

warm front

warm air

Catastrophic Blizzards

A severe blizzard has winds of 45 miles (72 kilometers) per hour or greater. Temperatures measure 10° Fahrenheit (12° Celsius) or below. Those conditions produce extreme wind chills.

In severe blizzards, visibility can be reduced to zero. This is called a **whiteout**. The ground is white, the sky is white, and the air is white. Getting lost in such conditions is easy. Flashlights or headlights are useless. Light just reflects off the blowing snow.

Severe blizzards can drop 20 inches (50.8 centimeters) of snow or more. The winds can blow the snow into giant drifts. The sheer weight of the snow can cause roofs to collapse and electric lines to snap. If fires start, they can be difficult to fight because water may freeze in pipes and fire hydrants.

▼ During this 1997 blizzard, Indiana motorists had to leave their vehicles on the highway.

Roads can become impassable in a blizzard. Airport runways get buried. Planes cannot take off or land. Worst of all, people may lose heat in their homes just when they need it most. Power lines go down. Pipes freeze. Fuel deliveries end because trucks can't stay on the roads.

The Schoolchildren's Blizzard

It was January 12, 1888. A mild winter's day in the Great Plains took a turn for the worst. Temperatures dropped twenty degrees in just a few minutes. The winds grew stronger. Heavy snow began to fall. People were caught outside by the storm.

Many children were at school. Some students and teachers tried to brave the storm to make it home. Many became lost in the whiteout conditions. Some died just feet from their homes. In all, 235 people died. This blizzard became known as the Schoolchildren's Blizzard.

▲ **More than 200 people died in the "Schoolchildren's Blizzard."**

The Blizzard of 1888

The Schoolchildren's Blizzard wasn't even the worst blizzard of 1888 in the United States. On March 11, a late snowstorm began to pound the East Coast and the Atlantic Ocean. It lasted for nearly three days. More than three feet of snow fell in New York and New Jersey. Four feet or more covered Connecticut and Massachusetts.

Cities such as New York, Boston, Philadelphia, and Washington simply shut down beneath the storm. Fierce winds built up snowdrifts that reached 50 feet (about 15 meters) high. The drifts

trapped people in their homes, buried streets, and closed the railways. Telephone lines were torn to the ground.

More than 400 people died in the storm. Many of them were on the 200 ships that sank during the storm.

▲ The Great Blizzard of 1996 covered much of the East Coast in record amounts of snow.

The Great Blizzard of 1996

In January 1996, snow from a huge blizzard covered an area from Virginia to Maine. A dozen states were affected by the 1,500-mile (2,413.5-kilometer) -wide blizzard. Record amounts of snow fell in many areas. Schools and offices were closed from Baltimore to Boston. Why was the snow so heavy? The blizzard stayed in place for a long time. A cold air mass further north kept the storm locked in.

Everyday Science

Meteorologists can have many different jobs. They might report weather conditions and make weather forecasts on TV. They might study how storms are formed. Some meteorologists work to develop better early warning systems about the storms.

Meteorologists might collect information about how weather is changing. They study the possible threat of global warming, the long-term heating up of Earth's atmosphere.

The Great Blizzard of 1996 affected more than fifty million people. Travelers slept in airports, waiting for planes that wouldn't fly for days. In many streets, National Guardsmen drove heavy-duty Humvees to take people to hospitals. Road conditions were just too dangerous for ambulances. At least 154 people died because of the storm.

▲ A New Yorker clears a path during the Great Blizzard of 1996.

RECORD SNOWFALLS

City	Great Blizzard of 1996 Snowfall in inches (cm)	Previous Record Snowfall in inches (cm)
Philadelphia, PA	30.7 in. (77.9 cm)	21.3 in. (54.1 cm)
Newark, NJ	27.8 in. (70.6 cm)	22.6 in. (57.4 cm)
Washington, D.C.	24.6 in. (62.5 cm)	22.8 in. (57.9 cm)
New York, NY	20.2 in. (51.3 cm)	26.4 in. (67.1 cm)

Conclusion

Hurricanes, tornadoes, and blizzards can all be catastrophic storms. They can cause great damage and take many lives. Hurricanes combine the strength of the wind and the power of the sea into a destructive fury. Tornadoes leave a trail of destruction with the planet's most violent winds. Blizzards unleash a deadly mix of wind, snow, and cold.

Many catastrophic storms have struck the United States in the past. Many more will strike the country in the future. Scientists can't stop the storms from developing, but they can warn people before catastrophic storms arrive. Now fewer people lose their lives to storms than in the past.

Solve This Answers

1. PAGE 7: Math checkpoint:
A tropical storm.
To get this answer, add 40 to 25. Then compare the result (65) to the wind speed for each type of storm.

2. PAGE 13:
a. True. Add the figures for hurricanes Hugo, Agnes, Betsy, and Camille ($33,870,000,000). Then compare the result with the damage amount for Hurricane Andrew ($34,955,000,000).

3. PAGE 18:
a. 2%. Find the bar symbol for percentage of all tornadoes. Then look at the bar marked F4/F5.

b. 65%. Find the bar symbol for percentage of all tornado-related deaths. Then look at the bar marked F4/F5.

c. F2/F3. Find 30% in the bar graph. Determine which category of tornado it corresponds with.

4. PAGE 21: 877.

Math checkpoint: To get this answer, subtract 420 from 1297.

5. PAGE 23:
a. 0 degrees F.
b. −17 degrees F.

30

Glossary

atmosphere   (AT-muh-sfeer) the mixture of gases that surrounds Earth (page 7)

catastrophic   (ka-tuh-STRAH-fik) capable of causing great damage and loss of life (page 2)

coastal area   (KOSE-tul AIR-ee-uh) land that is near the ocean (page 3)

eye   (I) the calmer, quieter zone at the center of a hurricane (page 8)

eyewall   (I-waul) the wall of swirling clouds around the eye that is the strongest part of a hurricane (page 8)

frostbite   (FRAUST-bite) injury to body parts, such as fingers and toes, that are exposed to the cold (page 22)

hypothermia   (hy-poh-THER-mee-uh) a dangerous drop in human body temperature (page 22)

landfall   (LAND-faul) the place where a hurricane first passes over land (page 5)

meteorologist   (mee-tee-uh-RAH-luh-jist) a scientist who studies weather and climate patterns (page 3)

polar   (POH-ler) near the North or South Pole (page 24)

spiral bands   (SPY-rul BANDZ) the areas of clouds, wind, and rain on the outer edges of a hurricane (page 8)

storm surge   (STORM SERJ) a wall of ocean water pushed toward shore by a hurricane (page 8)

updraft   (UP-draft) a current of air that moves upward (page 16)

warm front   (WORM FRUNT) the leading edge of a warm air mass (page 24)

whiteout   (WITE-owt) a complete loss of visibility that can occur during a blizzard (page 25)

wind chill   (WIND CHIL) the combined cooling effect of cold air and wind (page 22)

Index